Let's Get Soci

Come visit us for ideas of fun learning activities you can do at home with your kids.

follow us

creativitybuilders

creativitybuilder

email us

hello@creativitybuilders.com
and receive a freebie!

Creativity Builders

MY JOURNAL

My name is ___________________________

and I am _______ years old.

THINGS I'LL NEED:

- Pencil
- Crayons or colored pencils
- A positive attitude
- Lots of imagination
- To do my best! ☆

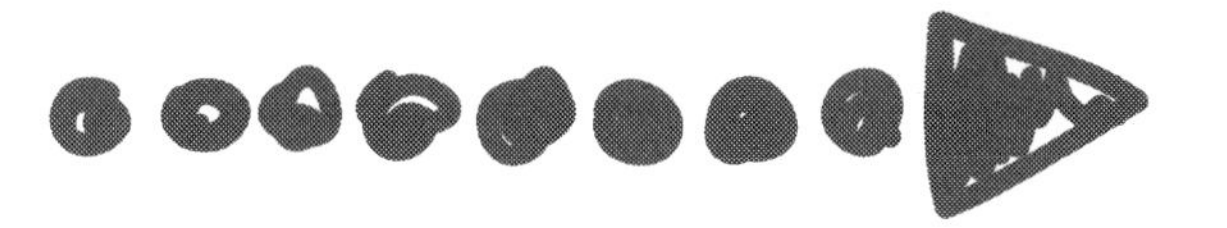

Imagine you place a seashell against your ear, but instead of ocean sounds, you hear the seashell talking! What does it say?

You won a trip around the world! Would you rather go on a submarine or a hot air balloon? Why?

Write a list of things you'd like to do this summer.

Would you rather be an expert surfer or an expert snorkeler? Why?

Explain to a new friend from another country how s'mores are made.

Would you rather play with snow or sand?

What could you do to challenge yourself this summer?

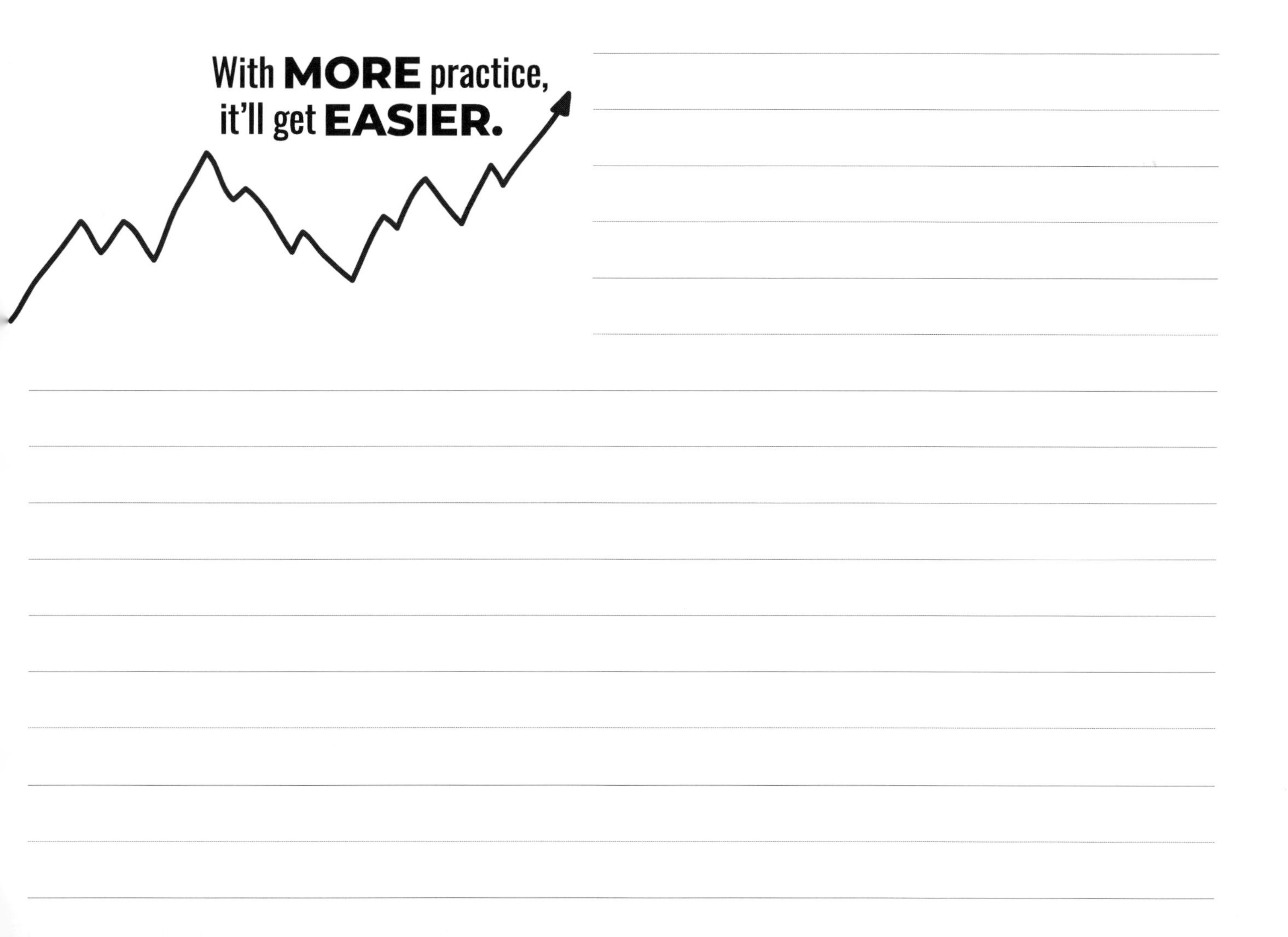

You are planning a campfire meal for your family and friends. What's on the menu?

If you must choose one ice cream flavor to have for the rest of your life, which one would you pick and why?

Your friend is learning how to surf for the first time. What can you tell them to encourage them to not give up?

Write about someone you love very much. What is he or she like?

Come up with a story with these words: lighthouse, lemonade, gassy, starfish and sunblock.

What is your favorite part about summer? What is your least favorite part about summer?

Describe one of your favorite photographs of yourself.

Your friend is visiting and keeps repeating, “I’m bored!” What 3 ideas can you come up with to have fun?

Would you rather spend the night at a mushroom cottage or a giant sandcastle? Explain your choice.

Santa Claus is finally taking a beach vacation! What kind of things would he do and who would he take?

What is your favorite insect?
Why is it your favorite?

Would you rather have the ability to glow like a lightning bug or catch things with your tongue like a frog? Explain your choice.

Pretend you are on vacation to a faraway place. Write a postcard to someone you love telling them about your trip.

AND
HAPPY
DEAR
AMAZING
HELLO
YOU

If you had a time machine, when and where would you travel to?

Describe a time when you made a mistake but learned an important lesson.

Which one would be worse to eat: worm ice cream or cricket cookies?

Create your own comic series.

What are some ways you can show kindness to people around you?

Come up with a brand-new summer holiday!
What would it celebrate?
What would people do?

If you found a bottle of pixie dust, how would you use it? Where would you fly and with whom?

List 3 ways rainy days can be fun.

Think of the last book you read.
What was your favorite part of the book? Why?

You are taking a nice nap in a hammock and something suddenly wakes you up! What happens next?

Explain what you would do if you were separated from your grown-up in a crowded place like a parade or big park.

Your favorite superhero has lost their powers for the summer. What kind of hobby do you think they'd enjoy while they're on a break?

Describe a time when you made yourself very proud.

Would you rather have a treehouse or a swimming pool? Explain your choice.

You are given a magical egg that can hatch any animal you wish for. Which animal would you choose?

Have you ever found a cool nature treasure (such as a feather, unique rock, pretty shell, interesting seed)? Where and when did you find it? What is it like?

If you could change one family rule for the summer, which one would it be?

Write about a time you got hurt playing outdoors. What happened?

What kind of summer job would you like to do when you are a teenager?

What is the best show on TV? Explain your choice.

Describe the perfect summer day. What would you do? How would you spend it?

You try a new soap, and your arms turn into crab claws. Describe your day.

Would you rather ride a bike through a forest or fly a kite in a meadow?

Describe fireworks to someone that has never heard about them.

Name at least 3 great qualities about you!

♡1 ____
♡2 ____
♡3 ____

Would you rather turn into an octopus or a narwhal for a day? Explain your choice.

Choose your favorite book.
Which character are you most like?

Pretend you are going camping with your family. Write a list of things you may need on your trip.

If it were possible, would you rather ride on a seagull or a seahorse?

It's a dark summer night and you are suddenly surrounded by beautiful sparkling fireflies. What happens next?

SUMMER WORD SEARCH

Q	L	X	V	D	L	T	H	H	Z	A	J
C	S	T	A	R	S	T	U	Q	X	U	T
L	Z	O	S	E	J	C	H	T	R	E	E
Z	R	G	R	F	J	U	R	Y	L	C	L
K	R	O	G	M	N	G	M	T	K	V	L
A	F	N	T	K	B	A	S	P	N	R	C
A	H	O	L	I	D	A	Y	Y	O	S	P
J	A	Z	N	T	C	X	L	H	W	A	F
T	Z	M	S	E	V	Q	K	L	E	Z	N
R	M	G	N	O	R	N	C	A	M	P	R
Y	N	D	T	I	C	Y	Z	L	E	S	X
E	M	Z	S	X	T	L	O	O	K	F	X

Find the hidden words in the puzzle.

ball	castle	tree
kite	stars	camp
forest	road	holiday
jump	look	know

SUMMER WORD SEARCH

L	I	F	E	G	U	A	R	D	I	C	N
K	S	U	N	G	L	A	S	S	E	S	N
U	N	U	Y	U	V	Y	G	V	S	C	C
T	H	A	N	K	S	Q	U	Z	L	C	O
C	I	D	X	S	P	L	A	S	H	X	O
R	M	B	K	S	C	F	L	Y	S	E	L
L	O	V	H	Q	S	R	E	M	K	A	N
G	P	N	M	G	F	S	E	L	U	A	T
F	L	O	A	T	H	M	A	E	A	A	O
L	A	B	Z	W	S	W	P	L	N	K	W
R	V	J	D	K	E	G	E	I	W	Y	E
P	I	N	D	C	L	O	U	D	Y	F	L

Find the hidden words in the puzzle.

cloudy
walk
float
towel
cool
fly
sunscreen
lifeguard
splash
lake
thanks
sunglasses

SUMMER WORD SEARCH

V	O	P	U	U	T	E	N	T	S	T	O
A	I	U	P	I	F	M	G	E	H	W	Y
Y	D	T	S	A	O	C	C	L	O	E	U
Q	S	K	E	E	W	F	A	S	R	A	R
L	R	I	R	T	T	R	M	Z	E	T	Q
T	U	E	J	Y	O	G	P	Y	Q	H	X
K	O	Q	V	C	I	C	G	A	G	E	Y
E	H	I	S	I	J	X	R	U	M	R	F
E	A	V	M	Y	R	W	O	G	K	H	L
R	T	I	M	E	W	K	U	U	V	W	X
C	O	Q	U	V	D	J	N	S	D	J	Q
U	M	J	I	M	W	Q	D	T	P	I	G

Find the hidden words in the puzzle.

week
august
time
weather

shore
hours
coast
coral

river
creek
tent
campground

SUMMER WORD SEARCH

R	R	W	H	Z	X	R	K	S	T	S	U	N	P	X
W	C	Z	J	I	Z	Z	M	I	A	N	V	O	W	O
Q	A	Q	H	F	P	I	D	O	M	N	P	X	I	M
P	S	T	H	D	C	Z	H	S	D	S	D	N	G	C
C	N	H	E	D	O	E	K	O	I	T	M	E	B	N
X	P	D	L	R	C	R	U	C	V	R	S	D	X	W
R	B	T	R	H	O	S	L	S	E	L	B	B	U	B
D	E	L	R	W	N	E	K	N	Q	J	X	O	U	M
H	Q	M	E	D	U	B	C	O	L	J	L	H	I	W
V	L	R	M	Z	T	I	X	I	Y	T	Y	A	O	G
N	I	I	J	U	N	K	K	T	B	A	Q	I	P	V
F	B	L	X	J	S	E	H	A	D	A	L	I	Z	E
U	M	B	R	E	L	L	A	C	H	Y	H	V	L	E
G	N	I	M	M	I	W	S	A	T	T	Y	O	I	G
K	O	B	T	J	U	Z	N	V	U	A	G	A	I	F

Find the hidden words in the puzzle.

bubbles
summer
vacation
umbrella

sun
water
coconut
popsicle

sand
bike
swimming
fireworks

SUMMER WORD SEARCH

Y	F	W	E	E	K	E	N	D	V	I	X	N	P	T
G	T	D	L	J	C	Y	J	Z	C	B	B	S	P	R
E	G	C	N	U	Z	O	T	U	U	B	Z	H	U	A
E	R	W	C	A	N	O	Q	Q	K	Q	T	D	B	T
L	P	E	B	B	L	E	F	I	L	N	T	J	H	S
V	R	Q	C	H	Z	S	Y	H	O	J	I	G	I	P
G	J	O	A	R	N	J	I	M	Z	C	Y	G	B	U
B	T	B	U	B	E	G	I	N	N	I	N	G	I	I
Y	D	H	X	N	E	P	D	X	C	J	G	U	X	J
R	A	V	W	A	J	U	M	E	V	C	Y	Y	U	U
N	O	S	A	E	S	O	E	V	E	N	I	N	G	D
Y	T	H	P	C	D	I	V	H	S	F	E	S	T	U
V	W	E	F	O	Z	M	P	E	Y	F	P	L	G	C
I	K	G	Q	Q	A	E	T	A	M	I	L	C	R	E
W	G	O	N	J	X	J	F	T	W	L	E	G	G	O

Find the hidden words in the puzzle.

evening	pebble	season
month	start	june
island	ocean	beginning
heat	climate	weekend

SUMMER WORD SEARCH

F	S	I	B	A	R	B	E	C	U	E	N	D	A	O
O	Y	A	P	I	I	O	W	F	C	X	E	J	F	G
W	I	B	I	C	Q	R	T	Q	K	B	B	D	E	P
X	J	V	J	L	M	I	P	Q	K	P	Z	D	B	B
D	Y	M	Y	X	B	E	Q	L	G	L	S	G	G	Y
C	T	J	G	M	V	O	A	F	W	J	P	V	E	D
F	I	T	X	H	V	H	A	N	F	R	A	I	N	T
X	N	Q	C	K	C	R	M	T	U	L	J	U	S	Y
G	S	A	B	D	K	K	V	D	Q	O	E	L	S	W
R	E	W	A	O	S	F	J	J	W	R	L	H	U	S
B	C	L	E	M	O	N	A	D	E	E	R	P	R	W
I	T	V	O	E	Z	K	L	I	H	U	E	H	F	A
E	V	O	O	J	S	H	Y	S	F	W	L	Q	I	V
G	A	E	Y	R	B	U	A	I	R	P	L	A	N	E
S	U	D	L	I	M	F	M	Y	U	N	Q	B	G	S

Find the hidden words in the puzzle.

rain
beach
barbecue
sailboat

surfing
insect
shells
airplane

chalk
lemonade
book
waves

SUMMER FOODS WORD SCRAMBLE

Unscramble the words below.

1. dlemonea ______________________________

2. sermso ______________________________

3. ecryhr ______________________________

4. trswyraber ______________________________

5. piecspol ______________________________

6. rguabrmhe ______________________________

7. ocnr ______________________________

8. mnoweratel ______________________________

9. nos neoc ______________________________

10. ctcuono ______________________________

11. eic aermc ______________________________

12. dtoogh ______________________________

SUMMER THINGS WORD SCRAMBLE

Unscramble the words below.

1. lrespsnirk ____________________

2. laecsntsad ____________________

3. tware ____________________

4. eumabllr ____________________

5. leffreiis ____________________

6. tten ____________________

7. iworfkesr ____________________

8. vwase ____________________

9. nshnueis ____________________

10. ocksbuln ____________________

11. ripmcaef ____________________

12. wtsismui ____________________

SUMMER PLACES WORD SCRAMBLE

Unscramble the words below.

1. aenco ______________________________

2. aelk ______________________________

3. rfsote ______________________________

4. ekcre ______________________________

5. torudoos ______________________________

6. dulganrypo ______________________________

7. gcdnrmuaop ______________________________

8. rkap ______________________________

9. olpo ______________________________

10. rrevi ______________________________

11. nislad ______________________________

12. hceba ______________________________

SUMMER VERBS WORD SCRAMBLE

Unscramble the words below.

1. tje kis ____________________

2. ashspl ____________________

3. lirgl ____________________

4. ursf ____________________

5. ekbi ____________________

6. etralv ____________________

7. wsmi ____________________

8. ifhs ____________________

9. asoeakrtdb ____________________

10. ipcgman ____________________

11. ediv ____________________

12. ikeh ____________________

THANK YOU!

We hope you loved our prompt book!
If you can spare a few minutes, leave us a few stars.☆
It really helps our small business!

Check out our other titles at:
author.to/creativitybuilders

Writing Prompt Books:
- 50 Writing Prompts for Kids: Grades 1-3
- 50 Writing Prompts for Kids: Grades 3-5
- 31 Spooky Writing Prompts for Kids
- 25 Christmas Writing Prompts for Kids: Grades 1-3
- 25 Christmas Writing Prompts for Kids: Grades 3-5

Elementary School Journal with Editing Checklist:
- Draw & Write Primary Composition Notebook: Grades K-2 | Dinosaur
- Draw & Write Primary Composition Notebook: Grades K-2 | Shark
- Draw & Write Primary Composition Notebook: Grades K-2 | Unicorn
- Handwriting Practice Paper: Exercise Book for Grades K-2 | Bacon & Eggs
- Summer Write & Draw Journal for Kids: Grades K-2

Scavenger Hunt Books:
- Go Explore Discover: Scavenger Adventure Book for Kids
- Go Explore Discover Beach Edition: Scavenger Adventure Book for Kids

Other:
- Trace Letters Handwriting Workbook: Alphabet Practice | Forest Animals Coloring Book
- My First Cookbook: 15 Kid Recipes for Pretend Play

Spanish:
- 50 Ideas de Escritura Para Niños (Spanish Edition)
- Anda Explora Descubre: Libro de Búsqueda y Aventura para Niños (Spanish Edition)

Made in the USA
Las Vegas, NV
07 December 2024